ParentSmart
Books™

Joytul and Confiden Parenting

D1408543

MAR 1 1 2004

Penny A. Shore

with

The International Advisory Council on Parenting

Penelope Leach, Ph.D.

William Sears, M.D.

Martha Sears, R.N.

Otto Weininger, Ph.D.

Canadian Cataloguing in Publication Data

Shore, Penny A.
Joyful & confident parenting

ISBN 1-896833-13-6

Includes index. 1. Parenting. 2. Child rearing. I. International Advisory Council on Parenting. II. Title. III. Title: Joyful and confident parenting. IV. Series: Shore, Penny A. Parent**Smart** Books.

HQ755.8.S52 2002   649'.1   C2001-901960-2

Published by The Parent Kit Corporation
2 Bloor Street West, Suite 1720
Toronto, Ontario M4W 3E2

Printed in Canada, by St. Joseph Printing Ltd.
First printing November 2001

1 2 3 4 5   05 04 03 02 01

Parent**Smart** Books
introduction to the series

Parenting has been my passion ever since the day my first child was born. This was, without doubt, an exhilarating and exciting event. However, it didn't take long to realize that with the birth of our child, we were taking on one of the most important jobs in life – and one for which we hadn't taken a training course. Furthermore, the baby didn't come with an instruction manual!

Now, my children have grown into happy, successful young adults and although my job is educational publishing, I have always considered parenting to be my most satisfying career. About four years ago, it occurred to me that I could combine my passion for parenting with my publishing experience. The idea was to produce a series of books designed to give new parents the very help and guidance I was looking for as a new parent. To develop the content, four of the world's leading parenting authorities were recruited to join me in establishing The International Advisory Council on Parenting. The members are; Penelope Leach, Ph.D., Otto Weininger, Ph.D., William Sears, M.D. and Martha Sears, R.N. The result of our combined efforts is the Parent**Smart** book series.

Despite the daily challenges faced by parents, there is probably no job in the world that matches parenting in terms of personal fulfillment and truly wonderful fringe benefits.

Parents who are properly prepared with the right tools and skills will have less stress and are likely to be more effective. That's why each book in the Parent**Smart** book series deals with one particular aspect of parenting. Taken together, the first six books in the series combine to provide a virtual "Parenting 101" course.

These books are unique in many ways. They provide you with a combination of expert information, interactive exercises and journals where you can record important information about your child. By having the full series available in your home, you will have easy access to the knowledge and support you will need to confidently handle most parenting situations.

There is another feature of the Parent**Smart** series that is very special. The experts don't necessarily agree on all parenting issues, and this can be confusing to parents who want their child to benefit from the best advice. We resolved this by having all members of The International Advisory Council on Parenting approve and come to consensus on the content.

A complete list of the other titles in this series, and a description of their contents, can be found at the back of this book. Parent**Smart** books are also a good refresher and primer for new grandparents, child caretakers and others in your extended family who will interact with your child.

Try to complete the questionnaires and exercises when you can. This will help you and your parenting partner to have a basis for communicating on the important issues and to be a better parenting team. The journals will provide records that you can enjoy and share with your children when they are older. "Tips and Techniques" are highlighted in the book to help you make immediate use of your new skills in every day situations.

I hope this book will raise your awareness about important parenting issues and give you the confidence to be a more effective and nurturing parent. Nothing can match the pleasure and happiness of seeing your children grow into fulfilled adults who are getting the best from their lives and whose friendship you cherish.

It has now been well-established that investing in your child's first three years will pay dividends in determining his or her future development. So, good luck with this stage and may your parenting adventure be one of the most rewarding experiences of your lifetime.

Penny Shore

dedication

To Joan, Eric, Jay and Amanda —
from whom I continue to learn.

Joyful and Confident Parenting

Table of Contents

The Two most Important Things a Parent can Give a Child are Roots and Wings

joyful and confident parenting

introduction

Being a parent will probably be the most exhilarating, demanding, rewarding and important challenge of your life. It is a lifelong commitment that is ever-changing and especially exciting today as new research tells us more and more about a baby's emotional and intellectual development. But your baby doesn't come with an instruction manual. Instead, you as a parent are expected to know intuitively what is best for your child. It's true, there is no one in the world who will know your child better than you do. But we can all use a little help and guidance. The important thing is to take the role of parenting from back-of-mind consciousness to front-of-mind – to parent in a self-conscious way.

The underlying premise in this book is that equipped with a deep knowledge of your child gained by investing time and energy, you are the expert. No one else will ever care for, know or love this child the way you do. No one else will want what's best for this child the way you do, and no one else will make the effort that you make to ensure this child gets the right start in life. The key, then, is for you and your child's caregivers to have the knowledge and skills, the confidence and support required to do the job the best way possible. You'll make mistakes and laugh at them later. But most of all, enjoy these first years with your child, have fun with her, and know that the gift of good parenting will last her whole lifetime.

Note: *Alternating between feminine and masculine gender in text can be confusing. So, for the sake of clarity, this book will use "she." The information applies equally to boys and girls, unless otherwise specified.*

meeting your newborn

Everybody's introduction to parenting takes place with the first newborn, and this newborn phase is an adjustment because you're both new at the job. But it can be an exciting, rewarding time for both of you as well. Newborns are extremely receptive to the world from the start. With this in mind, the physical management and care of your baby will be made easier.

Understanding your baby's point of view, watching her development, and learning what to expect, is the point at which to begin. Your mutual enjoyment in each other and your mutual effect on each other can have long-lasting results. If you "listen" to your baby, and learn to read her unique cues and signals, she will be your best guide on the parenting journey. Your love and attention to your newborn will be returned to you, and this loving relationship will form the crucial base for your child's healthy development.

NOTES

Your joy and confidence in parenting will depend on the fun and pleasure that you allow yourself to share with your child. Whether you are at home full-time or combining paid work with child-rearing, part of a couple or a single parent, your parenting role will make a difference. You will learn to compromise, laugh at your mistakes, deal with unnecessary guilt, and most importantly, grow as a parent.

Watch and listen to your baby. Listen to your own feelings and instincts. Be flexible. Find what methods work for you, your lifestyle and your child. Enjoy discovering who your baby is and caring for her as she develops, and discovering yourself as a parent.

Whether you are parents as a couple, a single parent of twins, or raising a child with special needs, and whether your baby is a first born or second born, one thing is sure – child development is a process and every baby will go through this process at her own rate, in her own way, in a certain order. It is not a race and you can't rush this process.

baby bonding

Bonding with your baby happens for some at the moment of birth, but for others, it takes more time. Either way, it is a learning process for both mother and father as they begin to know and love their baby. Whoever is going to be "mother" and "father" to this baby needs to come to terms with their new role. You need time together as a threesome, much like a honeymoon after a wedding. Plan for this time and make the arrangements necessary to enjoy it as much as possible. If there has been a difficult birth, or complications, you will need extra outside support to get you back on your feet, so that you can get on with the job of caring for and loving your new baby.

Your newborn is programmed with instincts and reflexes that enable her to survive and grow and learn. Her newborn behavior is unpredictable, but there are baselines to look for as you get to know her. If you know you are returning to work, allow yourself as much time as possible to adapt to this new person, and to let the love affair begin.

Touch and human contact are as essential to your baby as food, warmth and sleep. Her reactions to your handling her needs will guide you. If she gets what she needs, she'll know the world is a good place.

newborn basics

crying

Your baby's fussy periods may begin at around two to six weeks of age. Almost all babies will have one "fussy" or crying period of about 15 to 60 minutes, usually in the evening. It will take trial and error to see what comforts your child – all babies cry, but temperaments differ. The amount of crying usually decreases at around four months, when she becomes more socially interactive and more easily soothed.

Think of this crying as baby's first language or her way of communicating her needs to you. It's up to you to do the detective work to figure out why she's crying. Soon you will learn her different cries, and your warm concern and attention to her needs will pave the way to a foundation for her feelings of security and trust. You can't spoil a newborn. So don't hesitate to pick her up and comfort her.

physical characteristics

Newborns usually weigh between six and nine pounds and are on average 18 to 21 inches long. The head is typically one quarter the length, with a flat looking nose, a short neck and a receding chin. The belly looks swollen and the skin might appear dry. Hands and feet appear long, with arms hugged close to the chest and legs bowed, because of the position in the womb. The genitals of both boy and girl babies may appear large in proportion to the rest of their bodies. This swelling will rapidly subside.

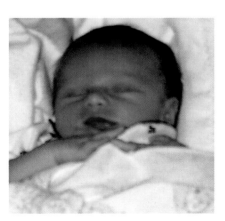

TIPS and techniques for comforting your crying baby

- Massage her back or tummy, or stroke her lightly and pat her back.
- Simulate rhythmic sounds and movement that imitate the baby's experience in the womb, for example softly humming with the baby in a carrier.
- Offer the breast or bottle. Some babies are soothed by sucking even if they're not hungry.
- Movement such as rocking, riding in a car, swinging, and walking, is one of the best baby soothers.
- Sounds such as gentle singing, soft music, or other "white noise" such as a dishwasher, vacuum, washing machine or humidifier, can lull a baby.
- Babies may need to feel the comfort of being swaddled snugly in a blanket or being put in a baby carrier.
- Check to see if something in the baby's diet is irritating. What mom eats affects the breast milk and can disagree with the baby.
- Less stimulation. If a baby is overstimulated by too much handling and interaction with too many people, she may need quiet time in a calm environment.
- Skin-to-skin contact and warmth are very soothing. Rub her with a warm hand, or hold her against your bare chest while you feed her.
- Try combining a variety of techniques. Sing as you rock the baby in your arms.

eating

NOTES

Newborns require as much breast milk or commercial formula as they want. They don't need solids until at least four to six months of age. After the first week, most babies gain approximately six to eight ounces a week no matter what kind of milk they get. Feeding a baby is not an exact science, because every baby will vary in her food needs and will adjust her food intake accordingly. You can trust her appetite as long as she is offered as much as she wants, when she wants it.

sleeping

Newborns sleep an average of 16 hours a day (with lots of individual variation) for short stretches of about two hours at a time. Some catnap for shorter periods and some sleep for longer periods. When it comes to your sleep, you can count on it being interrupted for a few months at least. Grab sleep when you can get it and know that "this, too, shall pass."

eliminating

Baby's first stools can look alarming – a meconium that is greenish black – but don't worry. This usually lasts only a couple of days. Stools for the next while tend to be greenish brown, loose and frequent. After the first month, this slows down, but frequency and consistency will vary greatly depending on whether your baby is breastfed or bottlefed. There can be variations from day to day in stools.

A new baby can urinate very often, even every hour. This is a sign that she is well hydrated. If the baby has not wet herself for more than a couple of hours, keep track of this. She may need more fluids – or may be starting a fever. Check with your doctor.

POINTS TO REMEMBER

■ Listen to your baby and let her be your guide to reading her unique cues and signals.

■ Development is a process that every baby goes through at her own rate, in her own way.

■ Touch and human contact are essential to your baby's healthy development.

■ Think of crying as her first "language" and her way of communicating her needs to you.

■ You cannot spoil a newborn — don't hesitate to comfort her.

from couple to family

The transition from "couple" to "family" can be stressful, it's true, because of the lifestyle shift that results. There is a delicate dance as you each come to terms with the transformation and its impact on almost every aspect of your lives. Sleep (and the absence of it), sexual intimacy, career ambitions and the need for mutual support – all these change once you have a child. Everything is brand new. Parenting is by nature a process of change – as your child grows, her needs shift and your roles evolve.

In this whirlwind of change and excitement, parents seldom have the time to nurture their relationship. The first year of your baby's life sometimes leads to both physical and emotional exhaustion and stress. It's critical during this time to keep the communication lines open. If you feel you need help, talk to friends, family or even a safe and objective professional. Don't let problems get out of hand.

1. **Take time with each other to share your feelings and express your needs.**

   Schedule time to enjoy each other. There is so much you are experiencing – joy, wonder, anxiety – that you must slow down to allow yourself time to absorb it all. Talking together will help you do that. Make it a priority from the start by setting specific times on your calendar to share time together. Even if it's only once a month, it's a reminder that you need and support each other.

2. **Adopt a team approach. Remember that you share the same responsibilities.**

   For example, no matter which one of you is actually carrying out a particular responsibility – a discipline situation, for instance – both of you should share in the discussion and decision-making about how it will be done. Whether a job change for either partner is right for the family at this time also needs to be a joint decision. Knowing that your partner supports you, instead of feeling alone throughout the day, is a result of shared emotions and responsibilities. By understanding what each of you has to offer your child – and each other – you can help shape and modify the atmosphere and parenting style you want to have for your family.

3. **Recognize each other's strengths and weaknesses.**
   We learn from and adapt to each other. By being able to depend upon your partner to be both a loving critic and a supporter in a relationship of trust and balance, you can grow as an individual and as a parent. As parents, it is your responsibility to set the tone for healthy growth and development in your family.

avoiding some parenting pitfalls

Becoming a parent is an evolving, wonderful growth process you and your partner can enjoy together. As you adjust to your new role as mom or dad, your baby brings changes into your lives. You only had yourselves to worry about before, but now, with the new responsibilities, feelings and relationships, you have to do some preventive work to avoid possible pitfalls.

The first step is talking. Both of you have attitudes about parenting that you may not have discussed with each other. Parenting will inevitably raise many issues on which you may take different positions. Find out how your partner feels by talking about such key issues as:

- each of your roles in caring for the baby

- doing chores in the house

- family budget and spending priorities

- feeding your baby

- returning to work

- the role of grandparents and other members of your extended family

- how your parents brought you up and how you want to raise your child

- where you expect to get advice on parenting topics

- how you will deal with crying, night waking, discipline

- your hopes and dreams for your child

On these topics you might agree or disagree, but you must respect each other's opinions and search for common ground. The way you communicate as a couple will have a strong impact on what kind of parenting team you become and, in the long run, will influence your children as they watch the two of you exchange ideas and express opinions.

The new family dynamics take time to settle into. You have to be flexible with each other and creative in finding time together, for intimacy, nurturing and support. Fatigue, stress and hormonal changes all play a part in how both partners get back to meeting each other's needs.

Balancing parenting and your relationship as a couple requires careful consideration, but the challenge will soon be met and you will have an even richer unit – your new family. Flexibility and a sense of humor may help you through this time.

Here's to the new baby, who as the parents will soon find out, is the perfect example of minority rule.

ANONYMOUS

redefining yourself

mothers

As a new mother, not only has your situation changed but so has your identity. If, for instance, you joined the out-of-home work world, you're now looking at life through new eyes, the eyes of a mother. The most important question to ask – before "What should I do?" – is "Who am I now?" Your pre-birth world view was the touchstone of all your previous decisions. Now, as a new mother, you will have to re-examine and re-define all areas of your life on new terms. How do I feel now about career and family? Are the goals I had before my child's birth still meaningful? What are my agreements with my partner about parenting? Is my anxiety telling me it's too soon to go back to work? Can I do everything I've always wanted and still be the mom I want to be?

Re-examine your goals and choose the most important ones to pursue; some now, some later. As you develop and enjoy your new identity, new answers to old questions will begin to come more easily.

fathers

You are going through your own version of "new eyes" and you are taking on new responsibilities, too. Men often forget to ask, "Who am I now?" as they rush to the solution of "What do I do now?" Talk to your partner about what kind of parent you want to be, and during the moments in between diapers, rocking chairs and careers, continue to discuss "Who am I now?" as well as "Who are we now?" As you continue to ask and answer these questions, your child will grow in a home where respectful conversation about current personal needs, wishes and choices are common-place. As your baby grows and matures, she will be asking herself these same questions. This modeling of good communication will help her choose, and care about, what means most to her. And it will be a style she can return to with trust and confidence as she grows into adulthood on the individual path she will follow.

POINTS TO REMEMBER

- Couples have to take the time to talk about their feelings.

- Both partners in a relationship have strengths that, when combined, make for a stronger parenting team.

- Both parents experience a shift in priorities as a result of their new roles.

- There is a shift in ways of doing things as you change from being a twosome to becoming a threesome with your baby.

the parenting team

it takes a village to raise a child

This famous African proverb is an eloquent expression of the kind of support network that best serves parents trying to raise a happy, healthy child.

With increasing demands on parents' time, pressure for mothers to return to work, and the trend to more geographically mobile families (including grandparents), this wisdom is more valid – and less possible – than ever before. We are less likely today to have older generations to help us out, and urban life does not lend itself to this kind of community spirit.

It is important, then, that you make an effort to create that "village" for yourself. If you discover, for example, that you have much in common with other parents in your prenatal class, stay in touch with them. Give yourself a way to discuss your anxieties and joys with others in similar situations. Or perhaps, a neighbor, or an acquaintance from your strolls in the park with your baby, can become your friend. Support groups and classes for new parents are other great ways for you to meet people. The village may no longer be an actual place on a map, but it can be a very real place in your life.

you and your partner

It's actually rare for couples to talk about child-rearing issues or their individual approaches to parenting before they have children, so it's no wonder that your partner's

unique approach to parenting can come as a surprise to you. You can each be competent and loving people, while having conflicting views on how to deal with specific parenting situations.

The reality is that you're two different people, with two different backgrounds and childhood experiences. But you don't always have to agree! Your child will learn to adapt to your different styles. And your different approaches will allow for creative problem-solving. As long as your basic parenting philosophy is similar, you will be able to negotiate your minor differences.

If you share the basic attitude that parenting is built on a mutually loving and respectful relationship between you and your child, and that your goal is to help her grow toward independence, she will be comfortable with your different styles.

Here are some ways to strengthen your parenting team.

1. **Share Your Childhood Memories.** Understand where your "knee-jerk" parenting responses come from. Many of our parenting beliefs and practices come from the way we were raised. Talk about your different family experiences and histories.

2. **Communicate Constructively**. Our parenting beliefs are deeply felt, but in a conflict situation, accusations and blame are destructive. Learn the language of respect, negotiation and influence.

   - Avoid Put-Downs and Blaming. Make it a discussion, not an attack. Frame it as an exploration. Ask questions that will lead to several possible options rather than one locked in solution.

   - Don't Oversell Your Point. Change takes time. Discuss the point and let it go.

   - Recognize Your Partner's Right to Choice. Your partner may not buy your parenting viewpoint – you have to respect that.

   - Focus on Important Issues. Decide which issues are really important and those you can let go.

   - Pick Your Moment. When you don't agree, it is important to talk, but not in the middle of the action. Wait until later, when you're both ready and willing to talk.

3. **Agree to Disagree in Private.** Try to present a united front and discuss your differences in private. Respect the other parent in front of your child. Respectful debate is positive, but open conflict is extremely distressing to children.

4. **Respect Each Other's Strengths.** Your partner's strengths can compensate for your weakness – learn to build on each other's good points.

5. **Find Common Ground and be Consistent on Important Issues.** Ground rules and limits should be understood and shared. Children need some consistency with discipline, bedtime routines and family "rules." Compromise and give-and-take will often work. After the discussion, make sure you both know what your policy is, so you can be consistent.

mom needs care too

It's not possible to care for your new baby or your partner if you feel neglected, overstressed and overtired. The most important person in your baby's life is you! Figuring out how to meet your newborn's needs takes time, energy and love, but you also have to get your share of nurturing.

physical recovery

Your postpartum weeks will be extremely busy tending to the needs of your newborn, and often there doesn't seem to be a moment to think about your own needs. Naturally, every new mother experiences a lack of sleep with her baby waking often during the night for feedings. It's important for you to meet your own physical needs such as sleeping, eating and exercising.

A full night's sleep is next to impossible during the first months of your baby's life, so it's important to rest whenever you can. Try to nap or relax when your baby naps. Let your partner or other caregiver spend some time with the baby, so that you can have a break.

> No one can make you feel inferior without your consent.
>
> ELEANOR ROOSEVELT

Make sure that you are eating well-balanced, nutritious foods to maintain your energy. Have healthy snacks of fruits, juices, nuts, cheese and yogurt.

After childbirth, getting your body back into shape is important. But remember, it usually takes a few months to lose that extra weight. Allow time for your body to recover, especially if you have stitches. For the first two weeks exercise should be light, increasing gradually to moderate activity to help your recovery.

Daily exercise, even a ten-minute walk, will help tone your body and increase your strength and energy. Getting outdoors with your baby in her carriage will also clear your head, decrease stress and help you sleep better.

Begin with gentle pelvic exercises as soon as possible, then move on to moderate exercises of the abdominal muscles when you're feeling up to it. Wait at least six weeks before doing any strenuous aerobic activity. As your body feels stronger, increase your exercises to low impact aerobics, such as walking, swimming or cycling. Many communities have mother and baby fitness classes.

emotional adjustments

Whether you're at home full-time or balancing home life with going back to work, you probably did not imagine how much time your new baby would take up in a day. Communicate to your partner about how you feel in your new role with the baby. Share the experience and enjoyment of parenting. If possible, try to find a relative or friend to stay with your baby for a short time so that you and your partner can have time out together.

After the excitement of giving birth, you may experience some depression or "baby blues." This postpartum sadness is normal and can be caused by a variety of factors, including changes in your hormone levels after birth. Other contributing factors include fatigue and the strain of meeting the many needs of your newborn. Talking to your partner, friends and other mothers about your feelings will help. Parenting and infant programs, as well as drop-in centers, are also available for support.

A more serious, but much less common, disorder called Postpartum Depression requires professional consultation. If your depression lasts more than two weeks, make an appointment to see your health care professional.

 **and techniques for new moms**

- Don't be afraid to ask for help if you need it – from friends, family, support groups or a professional. It will be better for you and your child.

- If you need a break, take some time out with your partner or a friend.

- Develop a support network or a communal baby-sitting co-op.

- Get some exercise – walks or a post-pregnancy exercise routine. Even 10 minutes a day will help. Use common sense and start slowly. Stop if exercise causes pain or dizziness. Consult with a health professional or fitness consultant.

- Let yourself fall in love with your baby. Every baby needs someone who's madly in love with her.

- If you can, sleep or rest when your baby does.

- Prioritize household tasks. Let some of the low priority ones go for awhile and, when possible, delegate some to others.

- Go with the flow. Forget schedules and efficiency. Your baby is generally not predictable and you can't work on the rest of the world's timetable when you've got a newborn.

- Enjoy your baby today – don't wish these early months away.

- Give yourself time to adjust. Nobody knows how to do everything for her baby overnight.

- Remember the newborn phase is short. Don't draw conclusions based on this brief period. Eventually, you'll get a full night's sleep again.

dad's role

New fathers today are taking a hands-on, active role in parenting. It's important to remember that the strong foundation for your new family is the partnership between mom and dad. And this relationship needs careful maintenance now. Use this time to put a little extra effort into couple maintenance while mom is adjusting to her responsibilities with your newborn.

All parents go through major changes once a newborn baby arrives. This period includes the joy of getting to know your new child, as well as the demands of feedings and night waking. It leaves less time and energy for your relationship with your partner. The mother's focus, especially if she is breastfeeding, is on the baby, and you may wonder how your role with your baby will unfold. It's normal to have mixed emotions about your new responsibilities as a father. As you adjust and gain confidence, nothing will come close to the joy and love you begin to feel for the newest member of your team.

 **and techniques for new dads**

- Take time off work and stay at home with your new family as long as possible.

- Pitch-in with meals, household chores and errands.

- Talk to and listen to your parenting partner. Show her your admiration for her new role as a mother.

- Discuss baby's feeding issues, night waking and crying with your partner to make sure you both are on the same wavelength.

- Limit visitors at the beginning to relatives and close friends.

- Support breastfeeding. Bring the baby to your wife and stay with them during some feedings.

- Bond with your baby. Cuddling, massaging, bathing and changing diapers are things that dads can do from day one.

- Let baby's mom sleep whenever she can. Help her to take some time off to be with friends.

- Develop a network of friends and relatives who can lend a hand, so you can have time out together as a couple.

- Remember your wife's physical recovery takes time; your sexual relations will improve with your loving care and sensitivity to her needs.

- Be flexible; maintain a sense of humor, have fun and enjoy the unique rewards of mutual love with your baby.

Men who are more involved in newborn care usually have higher, long-term self-esteem as a parent. You have an important role to play. You provide key support for the new mother, act as gatekeeper for family and visitors, and can pitch-in wherever possible in your baby's care and household chores. Being part of the team at the very start lets your partner know that the parenting will be a shared, companionable experience. Mothers can become very isolated as they care for their infants. Dads can let them know that they're not alone.

grandparents' role

Grandparents, whether living nearby or out-of-town, can play a major role in the enrichment of your baby's life. Of course, this grandparenting role depends strongly on the existing relationship that you have with your parents. If you have grown up in a loving home, communicating with your parents, chances are that they will blend easily with you and your partner in the care of your baby. This will no doubt make it easier for you to maintain your family's equilibrium. After years of feeding, disciplining and educating their own children, grandparents can now experience the joy of playing with and spoiling their grandchildren. But when you consider

that there can be seven or more people in the mix —
two parents, your baby and potentially two sets of
grandparents – it becomes very apparent how complex
this teamwork can be.

By having an open dialogue with your parents, you can let
them know the support that you need early on, such as
help with feedings, changing diapers or giving you some
much needed time out. Communicating to your parents
how you and your partner feel about various parenting
issues will help to bridge the generation gap. And by all of
you being consistent, your child will not become confused
by getting mixed signals. How you discipline your child
may differ from how you were disciplined, but as long as
these issues are discussed, grandparents can enhance your
child's care.

It's also important for you to establish some guidelines or
rules, particularly if grandparents live nearby and spend
a lot of time with their grandchild. Openly discussing
issues such as limiting cookie treats, handling crying, TV
watching, bedtime and safety will cause less disruption
later in your life. On the other hand, if grandparents live
out-of-town and visit infrequently, these rules can be
relaxed to accommodate their limited time. If your mother
wants her grandchild to stay up later than usual one
evening to join in the family fun, let her. And an occasional
sweet will not hurt your child. The warm, loving, grandparenting care far outweighs any rule you may have.

POINTS TO REMEMBER

- Your parenting team can be strengthened with effective communication.

- Respect your parenting partner's strengths and allow for different perspectives on a situation.

- Moms also need to look after themselves so that they have the energy and patience for their new baby. Ask for help if you need it.

- A "hands-on" dad in the first few months will be a more effective parent long-term.

- Grandparents can enrich your baby's life – and give you the support you need.

if you are a single parent

Research tells us that almost one in three marriages in North America ends in divorce or separation – and this statistic does not include informal separation, single parents who have never had a spouse, or marriages where a parent is single as a result of the death of a spouse.

Whether you are parenting alone, co-parenting with an ex-partner, or step-parenting with a new partner, the same parenting approach applies. Building your team, creating support, and communicating your parenting goals and attitudes to everyone involved with your children is more important than ever.

Try to adopt a parenting approach that is right for you. Without the help of another parent to make decisions, you will benefit from a high level of awareness and sensitivity to your child's needs. The added self-confidence you have in knowing your child well will help you make the right decisions by yourself.

It is important that you learn to pace yourself and are able to relieve yourself of some of the stresses of parenting alone. More than anything, your child needs someone who is relatively rested and happy to care for her. If you take occasional breaks from your routine, you can recharge and step back, allowing yourself to derive pleasure from what can be a tiring and stressful undertaking.

Being a single parent can be difficult and sometimes lonely, but do give yourself credit for being there for your child, and doing the best you can to create a good world for her to grow and develop in. If you find yourself asking, "Am I doing enough for my child?" you're sharing an uncertainty every parent sometimes feels, even those who are married and appear successful. It isn't just that there's no such thing as a perfect parent, it's also that a tendency to feel guilty is probably felt by every parent.

getting the support you need

Life as a single parent is a continuous challenge. But, on every step of the way there is help available. Friends and family members usually are the first line of support. Additionally, you can check with your family doctor, public health department, or the phone book for local support organizations. If you have access to the Internet, take advantage of it, using "parent" and "support group" as key words. Without the support and relief a helpmate can offer, a single parent can lose perspective, even hope. It is absolutely crucial that you seek out other individuals who can lend a hand, an understanding ear, and the wisdom from their own experiences. Make a list of the people in your life who can help you.

helping your child cope

You may not have a good relationship with your child's other parent, but try to keep your former partner involved in the mutual care of your child. It is beneficial if your child sees that you have an on-going communication with the other parent. Your child's emotional reality – maybe even her home base – will change, too. She will react to the absence – or worse, loss through death – of a parent, and will need help to cope with this loss. Divorce makes children unhappy – even if their relationship with the parent who leaves has been distant – and she may become extra clingy.

Try to facilitate, to the extent possible, your child's ongoing contact with the non-custodial parent. It will contribute to her long-term security and happiness. She needs to see and believe that both of you are available and are all right.

My Support Network

1. _____

_____

2. _____

_____

3. _____

_____

4. _____

_____

5. _____

_____

6. _____

_____

7. _____

_____

8 _____

_____

9. _____

_____

10._____

_____

CASE STUDY 1

When Nicholas turned five months, Monica decided she had to reach out. Being a single mom, the first few months had been hectic and demanding, but with her mother's help, she had managed. Now she was beginning to feel alone and isolated. She didn't really know anyone else who was at home with a child and she felt deprived of adult companionship. Her whole life seemed to revolve around her baby's schedule. Then one day, she noticed a sign posted at the local children's bookstore advertising a new play and support group that had just started at a nearby school. Intrigued, Monica took Nicholas the next day for a look around. To her delight, after less than an hour, she enjoyed several conversations with a number of other stay-at-home parents and found out about a special program at the museum, a support group for single parents. As Monica made some new friends, Nicholas, too, seemed to fit right in and soon was happily playing.

You have to expect things of yourself before you can do them.

MICHAEL JORDAN

 **and techniques for the single parent**

- Take some time to look at the new you. Whether you have gone through a separation, divorce or lost a spouse to death – you have changed. Admit some new limitations, begin to accept them, and grow in a new direction.

- Take some time for yourself. As a single parent you need more than ever to stay healthy – both in mind and body – to be there for your child.

- Take time for friends and family.

- Learn to say "no." Demands, made on you by your child or others, that you can't meet, need to be dealt with firmly.

- Don't forget your own emotional needs. Make a list of creative ways to vent your emotions and get the nurturing that you need.

- Seek and accept help when you need it. Friends, family and support groups can lend a hand and even barter caretaking help.

- Take time to listen to, enjoy, and have fun with your child. She will have extra emotional needs at this time and will need your sensitivity.

- Understand that an ex-partner may parent differently. Communicate your style to your child's other parent and try for some consistency on big issues.

POINTS TO REMEMBER

- Learn to pace yourself and find relief from some of the stresses of parenting alone.

- Seek out other individuals who can lend a hand, an understanding ear, and the wisdom from their own experiences.

- It is beneficial if your child sees that you have an ongoing communication with her other parent.

One kind word can warm three winter months.

JAPANESE SAYING

the foundation of joyful and confident parenting

Before you can build a house, you need a solid foundation. And before you can create a happy and healthy family, you need a positive, affirming environment in which your family can grow. Very often parents arrive at this new stage of life facing a bewildering array of changes they have barely considered. And it is no wonder, preoccupied as they have been with the pregnancy and the birth.

The best relationship with your child is a loving one, grounded on respect, trust and affection. No matter how old your child is, if you listen to her messages and respond to them honestly and with love, she will realize that she is important to you, and that you are willing to devote energy, time and love to her... because she is worth it.

Your child is unique and will respond in her own way to encouragement, challenges, tiredness and stress, as well as to good and bad times. There are no pat answers. It is only by listening to, and learning from your child that you – the person who knows her best – will know what is best for her.

Tips and techniques for learning to be an effective parent

- It takes time and practice to learn new skills. Be patient and have confidence in your ability to do the best for your child.

- You can't have a perfect baby or be a perfect parent. Enjoy the everyday simple pleasures of raising your child today – the next developmental stage will come soon enough.

- The most important thing in your baby's development is the happy and secure quality of caretaking that you give her.

- Parenting is a changing, evolving process. You will make mistakes and learn from them.

- You will guide and protect your child in her development, but she will teach you things as well, about her and about yourself.

- You can re-prioritize things that were important to you. If a super-tidy house has always been crucial to you, learn to live with a little mess. Save the energy for nurturing yourself and your child.

- Give up preconceived notions of how your baby should be or how she should respond and accept her as she is.

- Spend the time to get to know and "read" your unique child. How does she express her feelings or frustrations?

- Learn to assess a situation and adjust your reactions to match your child's needs.

- Self-esteem grows in a baby who learns that her parents value her for who she is, without her "earning" it. Your interactions with your baby will help form her self-image for life. Loving and caring for her helps her realize that she is important to you and that she has self-worth.

- Continue to learn new parenting skills by reading and looking for support and wisdom from other parents and support groups.

- Adjust your expectations to your child's developmental stage.

parenting skills can be learned

Parenting skills are not inborn, but learned. Old attitudes, learned from how your parents parented you, have to be examined consciously and assessed to see how they fit in with you, your parenting partner and your lifestyle today. Effective parenting can be learned. It takes self-insight, desire, knowledge and practice.

your parenting style

No two people will have exactly the same parenting style. We all come to parenting with our individual family histories, our personalities, strengths and weaknesses. Whether you're conscious of it or not, you have a unique personal style of relating.

All of us have patterns of behavior which affect our relationships. These repeated patterns of behavior make up our unique style as it is perceived by others. Mothers and fathers begin the parenting journey with the complex interaction between their own two styles and then layer on the interaction with their baby, who brings her own temperament to the table. As you interact with your baby, you will learn more about yourself, your style and your partner's style. Although any behavior is also guided by the specific factors of a situation, your state of mind and stress level, you will have a style that is typical for you most of the time.

Children develop best when parents can achieve reasonably well-balanced parenting styles that combine plenty of warmth and nurturing with flexible but strong direction. It's important to keep enough flexibility to respond appropriately to a particular situation or to your child's temperament. Talk with your parenting partner and your child's other caregivers about their particular style. The combination of your different strengths and weaknesses, and your different personal styles, can be positive for your child if the relationships are based on good communication skills and understanding.

Becoming a parenting team means that you understand the consequences of each style and that you can enhance and strengthen one another. The better you know your own limits, abilities and strengths, the better you will be able to adjust your style to meet any situation.

Perhaps the **greatest** social service that **can** be rendered by **anybody** to the country and to **mankind** is to bring up a **family.**

GEORGE BERNARD SHAW

ten ways to build a healthy parent-child relationship

1. **Develop an atmosphere of love and trust.** Children will live up to expectations and good role modeling. Give them something to model and live up to.

2. **Always respect your child's feelings.** Her feelings may not always seem rational to you, but they are very important to her. If you belittle or shrug off her fears and feelings, she will feel misunderstood and unloved.

3. **Give your child plenty of affection.** Hugs, cuddles and affection are always important. Even when she's older, your child will appreciate the comfort and love contained in these gestures. (Though at certain phases, she may find some public displays of affection embarrassing.)

4. **Spend time alone with each of your children.** Give each child your undivided attention, even if it's just for a little while. Read a book together or snuggle and chat at bedtime. She'll appreciate having you all to herself and you will have the opportunity of staying in touch with her.

5. **Keep your promises and commitments.** Whether your promise is to take her to the park tomorrow or that she can have a snack later, live up to it. If you're not sure you can do it, then don't promise. Disappointment is hard to handle. Your child needs to know that she can count on you.

6. **Say you're sorry when you make a mistake or lose your temper.** Nobody's perfect – even you – and she should know that. By apologizing, you're establishing a level of honesty between you and your child, and demonstrating that you care enough to have her understand what you are feeling. And what better way could there be for a child to learn about owning up to her own mistakes?

7. **Play and have fun together.** Enjoying each other in play helps rekindle your love. Sharing good times will make the rough patches easier to handle.

8. **Create a child-friendly home.** Make an effort to ensure that your young child can move freely throughout your house without fear of damaging something precious and without fear of disapproval. Make sure your home is a place where she can be happy and comfortable.

9. **Express anger appropriately.** Show your child your own problem-solving skills and model how anger should be handled.

10. **Never hit your child.** This will only demonstrate that you will overpower her instead of teaching her the right way to handle anger.

Follow the Golden Rule: Treat your child with the respect and consideration with which you wish to be treated. By doing so, you will teach her that she is valued and respected, and provide her with an example of how to get along with others.

Your child needs to:

■ know she can depend on you for comfort

■ develop self-respect and respect for others

■ know she is valued, loved and accepted for who she is

a lifelong relationship

One of the great dividends of a healthy and supportive parent-child relationship is mutual respect and love that will enrich the good times and sustain you through the tough times. You are always a parent. The delight you take in your child's first word, the first halting step, will be mirrored years from now as you take pleasure in your adult child's accomplishments.

POINTS TO REMEMBER

You can strengthen your parent-child relationship by:

- showing plenty of physical affection
- setting aside time alone with each of your children
- respecting one another's feelings
- keeping promises
- having fun together
- providing a child-friendly environment

taking stock

Each of us brings a set of skills when we begin parenting. These skills are a combination of what you learned from your parents as you were being raised, the values you have developed since birth, and the information you gather as you prepare for parenthood. You might think of all these skills together as your parenting tool kit. It will be the first resource that you will draw upon as you strive to be the parent you want to be. No matter what stage you're at in raising your own children, there will be times when you will need to add some new tools to your kit. And if you are open to doing so, it will be to the advantage of both you and your child.

lifelong learning

As a parent, you will be called upon constantly to adapt to new situations. Parenting requires reflection and self-awareness on your part. That process begins now, no matter what stage you are at in this lifelong commitment.

Many of us don't take time to examine our backgrounds to figure out what will be useful and what might be harmful to our children. Now is the time to take an inventory of your parenting information. It doesn't matter if you're still awaiting the birth of your first child or if you already have two or more thriving and growing children. A survey of the techniques, methods, and underlying philosophies that you use every day with your child will be very useful.

Take a close look at what's happening in your family right now. Consider how you deal with conflicts and behavior problems. When conflicts are settled well and easily, how do you do it? Are there times when things seem to spiral out of control and never get resolved? Look at the circumstances in both of these situations. What was the difference between satisfactory and unsatisfactory

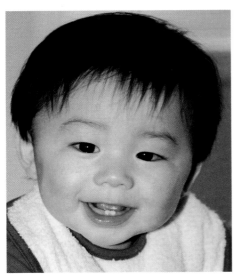

resolutions? Examine how your personality and your partner's affect the way you are handling situations. Is one of you, for example, highly demanding and results-oriented? Do you get impatient if things are not done when and how you want them to be done?

Consider your child's temperament and personality. This, too, is a crucial ingredient. Do you get into power struggles because one or both of you are difficult or stubborn? Do you find your nerves getting jangled because you like peace and quiet but your child is the rambunctious, energetic sort?

How were you parented? All of us are products of our own childhood, the saying goes, and nowhere is this more true than in the way we parent. Your own childhood is reactivated when you become a parent. Wonderful and not-so-wonderful memories are recalled, good and bad habits revisited. The difference is that this time, you are the parent.

Just as we use our parents as models (whether we like it or not), so, too, did they learn from their parents. What we do as parents may be based on the thinking of a few generations ago. While this can be a positive means of passing on the wisdom and experiences of our ancestors to our children, it is a fact that many wrong-headed methods, myths and misinformation are also passed down.

looking back

Your family is the source and protector of your children's physical and emotional growth and development, and it will have an impact on their quality of life, who they are and who they will become. What you can learn from consciously considering your own childhood and current experiences of family life – its structure, style, rules and communication – will help you create a healthy parenting style capable of adjusting to the ever-changing needs of all the members in your family.

how were you raised?

In order to explore your memories of your parents' child-rearing styles, you and your partner should take some time to answer the following questions. After you're finished, discuss your answers. By doing it together, you can open the channels of communication between you and your partner and learn about yourselves.

1. Was love expressed in your parents' relationship?
  Was anger expressed?

1	2	3	4	5
only negative feelings expressed		equal ability to express anger without denying love		only positive feelings expressed

2. How did your parents deal with disagreements and conflict between themselves? How did your family, as a whole, resolve conflict?

1	2	3	4	5
conflict not openly expressed		differences aired and amicable solutions found		conflict resulted in anger and disrespect

3. Was there direct and clear communication between your parents? Or were they communicating through unclear and ambiguous nonverbal signals?

1	2	3	4	5
"scrambled" communication that had to be decoded; saying "yes" but meaning "no"		open, non-blaming expression of feeling		constant misinterpretation and blame

4. What was your level of dependence on your parents as you were growing up? To whom did you turn for help as a youngster and as a teenager?

1	2	3	4	5
complete reliance on your family		healthy balance		had to rely solely on people outside the family for nurturing needs

5. When you left home, was it with the love, support and encouragement of your family? Have you stayed in touch and connected with your family since?

1	2	3	4	5
you felt pressure not to leave		you welcomed the challenge to enter the world as a young adult		you left before you were ready

6. When you left home as a young adult, did you have the confidence and trust in your own abilities to make it in the world?

1	2	3	4	5
you were intimidated and unprepared emotionally		you had reasonable confidence in yourself		you were overly confident and unaware of your new responsibilities

You are the bows from which your children, as living arrows, are sent forth.

KAHLIL GIBRAN

My Positive Childhood Memories

What are your best childhood memories? What are the experiences you had as a child that you want to provide for your children? Consider carefully what it is that you cherish about those times. Was it the closeness? The sense of security? The laughter? Was it, perhaps, the understanding, or the acceptance, you felt you received from those around you?

Looking at your answers to the above questions, make a list of the ways you believe your parents handled situations well.

1. _____

_____

_____

2. _____

_____

_____

3. _____

_____

_____

4. _____

_____

_____

5.

_____

_____

_____

6.

_____

_____

_____

7.

_____

_____

_____

8.

_____

_____

_____

Other memories

_____

_____

_____

_____

_____

_____

_____

_____

_____

_____

My Negative Childhood Memories

It is also important that you take stock of the times that you wish things had been done differently when you were a child. Try to recall the unhappy times and place them in the same perspective as the positive memories. Don't think of this exercise as trying to place "blame" on someone for something that happened so long ago. What you are trying to understand is what happened way back when, and then reach an understanding of how you can avoid those mistakes. Only by accepting that your parents were not perfect can you ensure that your family will be better served with a different set of parenting tools. And remember, all of us make mistakes. Without being judgmental, make a list of some childhood situations that you feel were not handled well by your parents.

1. _____

_____

_____

_____

2. _____

_____

_____

_____

3. _____

_____

_____

_____

4. _____

_____

_____

_____

5.

6.

7.

8.

Other memories

CASE STUDY 2

Angela and David had been married three years before their daughter Emily was born. They believed themselves to have compatible outlooks and expected to have similar parenting styles. That their styles are different was shown when the three of them were out for dinner one night. David and Emily, age 2, went ahead to the restaurant, where Angela would meet them after work. Not long after father and daughter arrived, Emily wanted to get down from her high chair to explore this interesting new world. David became increasingly agitated. Finally, he put his foot down and made it clear to Emily that they would have to leave the restaurant if she kept it up. Not surprisingly, she did. David got even angrier and was just about to leave when Angela arrived. Sensing that things were pretty tense between the two of them, Angela focused on calming Emily. She looked at the menu with her and finally passed her a piece of bread with a pat of butter. "There," Angela said, "She must have been hungry. That'll keep her busy for a few minutes."

David, perhaps worried that Emily might cause a scene in the restaurant, had tried to tell her what she could and could not do, or even feel. Angela, on the other hand, had recognized that Emily needed some attention that would calm her and give her something to do. Later in the evening, David realized that he had been reacting the way his father had years ago.

POINTS TO REMEMBER

- Parenting is a process of lifelong learning. As a parent, you will be called upon constantly to adapt to new situations.

- Consider how conflicts and behavior problems are dealt with now. What works... and what doesn't?

- Consider your child's personality and take the way she reacts to you as a guide.

- All of us are products of our own childhood and nowhere is this more true than in the way we parent our children.

making your home child-friendly

The time to babyproof your home is before your infant needs it. Babies' development proceeds by fits and starts. Some overnight accomplishments can take parents by surprise; that's how so many babies who can almost roll over one day come to roll right off their changing tables the next. The babyproofing of your home that you undertook when your child first started to get moving may not be adequate once she's on two feet. Think again about any safety gadgets that seemed unnecessary then; they may be badly needed now. If keeping a safe home is tricky for parents who are around all the time, it's far more tricky for people who are not. Make sure nannies, babysitters and relatives are briefed about safety issues. As her protector, it is up to you to ensure that your baby's learning environment is safe. Most accidents are preventable. Try to look at your house from your baby or toddler's viewpoint. Get down on your hands and knees to check how she views the world. By eliminating dangers without being overprotective, you can prevent serious accidents so that your child is free to enjoy exploring and learning in your home.

safety in the home

The following list contains some highlights for safety in various rooms in your house. It is by no means a comprehensive list. (See recommended reading at the back of the book.)

kitchen safety

• When you are cooking, use the back burners of the stove, with pot handles turned toward the rear to avoid burns. Use a stove guard so that your child can't touch the burners. Consider knob covers.

• Have a multipurpose fire extinguisher in the kitchen.

• Install smoke detectors on each floor of your home, and check the batteries regularly.

• Install safety latches on some cupboards and drawers, particularly those with harmful items such as knives or scissors.

• Lock up harmful household cleaning products, plastic bags and matches.

• Make sure appliance cords and tablecloths are not dangling over countertops, where young children can pull them down.

• Keep small appliances such as toasters and blenders unplugged.

• Use unbreakable glasses and dishes for feeding your child.

living room safety

- Fasten furniture, such as bookcases, to the wall to avoid them being pulled over. Remove unstable furniture.

- Cover the sharp corners on low tables. Cover glass tables that could shatter.

- Use safety gates at the top and bottom of stairways and safety plugs to cover electrical outlets.

- Use guards to keep children away from fireplaces and other heat sources.

- Keep plants, knickknacks and any mouth-sized items, which could cause choking, out of your child's reach.

- Check that the cords from table lamps cannot be pulled by your child. Tie up cords from blinds and curtains.

- Make sure heavy objects on shelves, such as a TV, are set back so they can't be tipped over.

bathroom safety

- Always test bath water with your forearm or the inside of your wrist to prevent burning your baby's skin.

- Never leave a child unattended in the bathtub.

- Never leave water in the tub when it is not in use.

- Use nonskid mats on the bottom of the tub and place childproof covers over cold and hot water knobs to prevent your child from turning on the water.

- Keep all electrical appliances away from water.

- Keep the toilet seat down.

- Keep toiletries, cosmetics, cleaning products and medicines with safety caps locked and away from your child.

- Disengage dead bolt locks and, instead, try to use a high safety latch to lock the door.

equipment safety

crib safety

Make sure your baby's crib meets safety standards. It should have non-lead paint and a crib rail with bars no more than 2-3/8 inches or 6 centimeters apart. Check for anything in the crib construction that could cause your baby to get stuck or pinch her fingers. The crib should have a firm, flat mattress that fits snugly into the corners. Crib bumpers should also fit snugly and be secured with ties. Remove the bumpers when your child begins to pull herself up using the crib rails. Make sure the crib is not near window blind or curtain cords to prevent strangling. Keep the crib away from other furniture which the child may use to climb out of the crib. Her toys, pacifiers, bumpers and clothing should not have a dangling string longer than 8 inches or 20 centimeters. Consider using a baby intercom if the crib is not near your bedroom.

---

safety alert

Research conducted in several countries suggests that letting your baby sleep on her back will reduce the risk of Sudden Infant Death Syndrome (SIDS), also known as crib death. Other recommendations include breastfeeding, as well as avoiding dressing your baby too warmly at night, not smoking during pregnancy, and not exposing your baby to second-hand smoke after birth.

---

highchair safety

A baby is usually ready for a highchair around the age of five months, when she can sit up with support. Make sure that her highchair has a wide base for stability and a tray that locks securely. Always use a safety belt to secure your baby in her highchair and never leave her unattended. The highchair should not be near hazards such as stoves, shelves, tables, counters, windows and dangling cords from blinds or drapes.

stroller safety

Select a stroller with a wide wheel base for stability and check to make sure it will not tip over when your baby leans forward or backwards or is in a relaxing position. Check latches and brakes for safety.

safety alert

- **Childproof your home before your child needs it – the goal is accident prevention.**

- **A cordless phone is a good investment so that you can move around your home to stay near your child when answering calls.**

- **Have the telephone numbers of the police, hospital emergency room and the poison control center near the phone. Remember, accidents may happen, so always have a first-aid kit handy.**

- **Keep on hand ipecac syrup to induce vomiting, but use only on the advice of the poison control center.**

- **Make sure that your child's relatives and other caregivers know and follow these safety procedures.**

car seat safety

Purchase a child car seat appropriate for your child's age, weight and height. Make sure that it meets current government safety standards and is installed and adjusted correctly, according to the manufacturer's instructions. Develop a strict set of "car rules" which include all passengers buckling up before starting the car engine. Use a child car seat only on a seat that faces forward and never put a child under age 12 in front of an airbag. Never use an infant carrier or an infant seat as a substitute for a car seat.

most common accidents
(newborn to three)

Birth to Six Months (Rolling and Reaching)

- crib accidents
- burns from adults' hot drinks or cigarettes
- falls off changing table or out of infant seat
- auto accidents

Six to Twelve Months (Crawling and Cruising)

- toy accidents: sharp edges, strings, mouthable parts
- grabbing accidents: burns from hot drinks, cuts from breakables
- highchair accidents
- pulling objects over on themselves
- falls against sharp table corners
- walker and stroller accidents
- cigarette burns
- auto accidents

One to Three Years (Walking and Exploring)

- climbing accidents
- unguarded water hazards such as: pools, ponds, bathtubs
- ingestion of poison
- exploring accidents: storage cupboards, medicine cabinets
- auto accidents

recommended shopping list for child safety products

- Car seat

- Nonskid rugs

- Intercom or baby monitor

- Safety latches for drawers and cabinets

- Doorknob covers

- Netting for railings and balconies

- Cushioned covers for tub faucet

- Tot-finder decals

- Safety plugs for electrical outlets

- Guardrail that fits under adult mattress

- Edge cushions for table corners, fireplace hearths

- Screen guards

- Stairway gates

- Cordless phone

- Rubber stripping for stairs

- Lid lock for toilet seats

- Flame-retardant sleepwear

- Fire extinguisher

- Stove knob covers

POINTS TO REMEMBER

- The time to babyproof your home is before your child needs it.

- Try to look at your house from your baby or toddler's viewpoint.

- Make sure that your baby's crib, highchair, stroller and car seat meet safety standards.

- Make sure that nannies, babysitters and relatives are briefed about safety issues.

child care issues

choosing child care

If you are returning to work, you will be entrusting your baby to the care of someone else. This is difficult for any parent. These decisions will require family discussion, investigation, and careful checking of alternatives. This material is introductory only and should be followed by your own detailed research. Making sure that your child is in a safe and healthy environment is the most important way to ease your mind. You will choose from three basic types of care.

individual home care

An individual cares for your child in your home. If this person is not known to you as a friend or family member, she or he should be checked for good references. You set the standards for a safe environment, nutritious food, and the emotional tone of your home. You want the caregiver to be a part of your team and to encourage the bond between you and your baby.

home or family day care

A caregiver looks after your child in her home. Check that your caregiver is licensed. In this case, the physical environment should be carefully examined for safety, a child-friendly atmosphere and cleanliness. Often, these caregivers have children of their own, or care for other children, in addition to your own. Arrange to meet the other children to ensure that the group is compatible. Discuss your parenting views with the caregiver to make sure that you are both taking the same approach. This care tends to cost slightly less than a day care center or in-home care, and tends to be more flexible and less formal.

day care center

Trained caregivers look after your child in a licensed facility. The fewer children assigned to each caregiver, the better. Check for the legally required ratio of children to adults. The ratio of children to caregivers goes up as the children get older. Look for a program with a child care philosophy similar to your own.

TIPS and techniques for choosing home day care or a day care center

- Your child needs respectful care.
- Visit the home or center two or three times, perhaps unannounced, to see how the children are treated and how they behave with the childcare providers.
- Ask for references.
- Check for number of staff relative to number of children.
- Talk to other parents who use this service.
- Look for clues to tell you how good the match is for you, e.g., level of interaction between the provider and the children.
- Stay involved. This will contribute to your peace of mind.
- Ask what staff turnover has been in the last year.
- Books, toys and ceremonies should be appropriate for your family's cultural background, and boys and girls should be treated with equal respect.
- Toilet assistance should be provided on an individual basis, not in a group situation or on a schedule.
- Physical space should be clean, warm, bright and cheerful.
- Look for outdoor play space in daily use.

CASE STUDY 3

Connie was a first-time mom with a beautiful six-week-old son. She had always assumed that when Jason turned three months old, she would head back to her job as a quality-control specialist in a large photo lab, a job that she had always enjoyed. Now she was not so sure. She realized she would like to spend a longer time at home with the baby. She didn't know what to do or even how to broach the subject with her husband Lee.

Lee, however, had noticed the anxiety in his wife and brought up the subject one night. Connie admitted to feeling torn, and they talked about their options. The next morning, before heading off to his job as a police officer, Lee said that he had thought about it some more and was sure that if Connie really wanted to stay home longer, then they could manage without her salary. Maybe they would take a cheaper vacation nearby instead of renting a camper and driving to the Grand Canyon. They could do the bigger trip another year, and it would be worth the wait if Connie could stay at home with Jason a little longer. And they didn't really have to move to a new house just because they had a baby. The house they lived in was fine.

factors to consider in choosing a play group or preschool

- Policy for parents' visits

- Your child's personality and individual needs

- His emerging interests, e.g., music, art, physical activities

- Timing, e.g., regular half-day program, or part-time program

- Your child's health concerns, e.g., allergies, asthma or any special needs

- Family situation, e.g., child needs a break from siblings

- Geographic location, cost and scheduling

- Program's philosophy

> Nothing is more difficult, and therefore more precious, than to be able to decide.
>
> **NAPOLEON BONAPARTE**

POINTS TO REMEMBER

- Making sure that your child is in a safe, healthy environment is the most important way to ease your mind.

- Care in your home means that you set the standards for a safe environment, nutritious food, and the emotional tone.

- When you look for care in someone else's home, make sure they are licensed, and that the atmosphere is friendly and the home is clean.

- Look for a day care center that has a program which shares your child care philosophy.

special situations

parenting children with special needs

If you have a child with special needs, you may sometimes feel overwhelmed. But most parents find that they can rise to the challenge, especially if they can be helped to attain the right attitude, get the support they need, and come to the realization that they are having a positive impact on their child's present... and future life.

Parents of children with special needs have to deal with a variety of different issues. By acknowledging your sadness, as well as your joy, as the natural reactions they are, you can come to grips more easily with the challenges ahead. While your special needs child may have a different set of attainable goals and expectations, her accomplishments are no less a wonderful source of joy and pride for you.

Your most important step now is to get the support you need. Talk to your family and friends about what you are feeling and what you need from them. People may find it hard to know what to say and may feel uncomfortable. They may wait to take their cues from you, so don't hesitate to ask for help or guidance.

Some parents find that making that initial contact is difficult because it implies some kind of acceptance of a condition they are not emotionally ready to accept. But it is precisely at this time when the support of others can be so valuable. Perhaps most importantly, other parents of children with special needs will show you methods that have helped them cope – and thrive. These parents, because they have their own emotional stake, not to mention commitment fueled and maintained by love, are often equipped with the most up-to-date and reliable information.

> # We are all pencils in the hand of God.
> **MOTHER TERESA**

TIPS and techniques for parents of children with special needs

- Stay in touch with your support network of friends, family and, most importantly, other parents of children with special needs. Don't allow yourself to become isolated.

- You are your child's advocate. Stay positive. Know how the support system works and practice creative problem-solving.

- Don't be afraid to stand up for yourself and your child.

- Work with educational and health professionals as partners.

- Help people to help you – let family, friends and professionals know your family's needs.

- Plan for your child's future. Recognize that there may be long-term care and financial issues.

- Look after your own physical and mental health – it will help you stay on an even keel.

parents of multiples

Being the parents of twins means double the work, it's true, but it can also be doubly rewarding. With advances in prenatal care, it is unlikely that you will be surprised with twins in the birthing room. It is worthwhile to seek out community support groups before the birth and attend as many meetings as possible before and after delivery. You will not find a better resource than other parents who are experienced in raising twins.

Naturally, with twins comes added responsibility. Good parenting teamwork is more important than ever. Indeed, with twins, the mother and father roles become blurred, and all the high-demand mothering tasks will have to be shared. If you are in a situation where that is not possible, it is imperative that you look for support. Allow any caregiver volunteers (be they grandparents, siblings, friends or neighbors) to pitch-in. They don't have to take on the high-intensity jobs, but – especially in the first few months – you will need an extra set of hands.

finding a support group

If you are interested in joining a support network for new parents or a play group where you can meet other parents with young children, check with your doctor or a public health department, as well as nearby schools, libraries and recreation and community centers. Some examples of support groups are Single Parents, Down's Syndrome groups and Parents of Multiple Births. See the back of this book for some national organizations that will provide you with further information. Don't forget that with today's technology, you can use the Internet to access current resources that are available in your geographical area.

POINTS TO REMEMBER

- Acknowledging your sadness and your joy will help you come to grips more easily with the challenges ahead.

- Get the support that you need.

- Check with your doctor or public health department, as well as nearby schools, libraries and recreation and community centers for a support network.

parenting myths and stereotypes

myth no.1

spare the rod and spoil the child

Surveys have shown that a large percentage of North American parents believe in spanking, and many of them regularly put their beliefs into practice. What these parents (some of whom believe in healthy, cooperative forms of child-rearing) don't realize is that all their best efforts can be undone by keeping this supposed parenting tool in their kit. Remember, as a parent, everything you do will be a model of behavior for your kids. The rule is to never, ever hit your child.

There are many alternatives to physical punishment that will help your children learn appropriate behavior. More importantly, they will also learn why. Positive, preventive discipline based on love, trust and understanding, not fear and humiliation, is what you need to strive for. After all, the goal is to equip your child with the necessary tools to go through life with inner discipline, and to be happy and fulfilled, capable and comfortable in expressing a range of emotions appropriately.

myth no. 2

you can "spoil" your child with too much attention

Children cannot have too much companionship, play, talk and laughter. A selfish and constantly demanding four-year-old is not that way because of too much attention. It is more likely she has turned out that way because she learned that this behavior is an effective means of getting the attention her parents have not freely given her.

Being attentive and affectionate with your child will not "spoil" her. Instead, it will give her the security and confidence to grow and learn. Your child needs you from the very start to show her that she is loved, valued, trusted and accepted. She needs to learn what is appropriate behavior, both by example and through meaningful limits. That way she will learn who she is and what she can be – and like herself because she knows you love her.

myth no. 3

your baby is trying to manipulate you

Most parents have heard, at some point, that they must let their babies cry because to pick them up would be to reward "bad" behavior and lead to spoiling. However, this is – one hundred percent – bad advice. Infants can't misbehave; they can only communicate their needs. Your refusal to respond may, in fact, teach your baby that she can't reach you, can't tell you what is wrong and that her needs will not be met. A parent's first challenge is to figure out what her baby needs and wants. Experts used to believe this was entirely the parents' responsibility and that children were simply passive individuals. Research over the last several decades, however, has shown that babies are "programmed" to shape their parents' responses. Cries, smiles and clinging are all "designed" to alert you to her needs. Body language, eye contact, even her cuteness are all keyed to the inclination of both parents to respond to cues.

myth no. 4

be tough because it's a harsh world out there

It has been said that the best way to prepare your children for life is to teach them about disappointment and hardship – and that it is your responsibility to do this. The thinking seems to be that by toughening them up now, they won't be hurt later. This is wrong. You prepare your children for adulthood by teaching them to be resilient and self-confident. And, you do that by teaching them that they are valued and worthy, that they are loved. Secure in that knowledge, they will be able to confront hardship and difficulty with greater ease than children who have been taught that it is a harsh world where no one can be counted on to support them.

myth no. 5

accomplishments and milestones – earlier is better

The timing of when your child reaches a specific milestone says nothing about her potential, her overall health and well-being, her likelihood of later success or her worth. Simply put, sooner isn't necessarily better. Many of us often behave as if the child who walks earliest will run fastest and the child who is rushed into reading – well before she might be expected to master it – will somehow be a better reader or even writer years later. Research has shown that this just isn't so. Instead, the competitive pressure, frustration and disappointment you may feel will be communicated to your child, and this, more than anything, can impede her progress by damaging her burgeoning self-esteem.

myth no. 6

formula is better than breast milk

Breast milk is the best thing for your baby. Mother's milk is what nature intended babies to have and has health benefits that no commercial formula can match. But it is important to understand that if you choose not to breast-feed, or cannot for some reason, you should not feel guilty. If possible, keep your options open by at least trying to breastfeed. One reason to start on the breast is that your child will get the colostrum your body produces right after childbirth. There is no artificial equivalent of this natural first food that contains essential proteins, minerals and important antibodies that will help protect your child's health while building her immune system.

What's important here is that you make an informed decision so that, knowing all the facts, you can decide what is right for you and then be happy and secure in the knowledge that you have determined what will work for you and your baby.

myth no. 7

fathers can't be emotional, loving parents

The biological differences between man and woman, father and mother, are facts of nature. These differences are not in themselves a problem. On the contrary, they are an advantage.

During the first few months of your baby's life, the roles mothers and fathers have with their children are fundamentally different. After all, the mother carries the baby to term, through birth and into breastfeeding. During the first months, your baby sees her mother (or a mother substitute) as her primary source of gratification and, early on, an extension of herself. In your baby's early days, it is up to the father to take on a supporting role and learn to hold, nurture and comfort his baby. You both can begin to bond with your child and, just as importantly, support and nurture one another. You can create and maintain the atmosphere in which the baby and mother can thrive. The father's role, although initially very different from that of the mother's, is also an active, supportive one.

More and more fathers these days are choosing to spend time and even stay at home with their children. Fathers can be loving and supportive, be involved on a daily basis and be as affectionate as mothers. For many fathers this may mean rejecting some of the parenting myths they have grown up with – and, likely, it will require a conscious decision to remove some acquired tools from their parenting tool kits, as we discussed earlier.

myth no. 8

children should be seen and not heard

Your children will benefit immensely from participation in your daily life, whether it is at the dinner table, in a family discussion or with guests in your home. By being allowed to contribute and respond to various situations and to give voice to their perspectives, your children will begin to learn about how we all get along and what is appropriate behavior in different scenarios. They will also learn that their thoughts and feelings are important. And you'll be surprised at what you learn from them as well.

myth no. 9

a good parent never gets angry

Simply put, impossible. There will be times when you are tired, frustrated or overwhelmed. No one can stay in control of his or her emotions all the time. It's okay for your child to see that you are angry sometimes, but she needs to know that she is safe and secure even when you lose your cool. By talking to her about it once you've calmed down, you will also teach her how she can deal with her own anger.

myth no. 10

statistical norms are a useful way to assess your child's growth and development

Your child – every child – is unique. Her birth weight, the rate at which she grows and develops, the milestones she reaches and when, are all her own. The notion of a statistically derived "average six month old" being a certain height and weight and doing certain things, is not a definitive guide. For although it is based on thousands of exemplars, each child is unique. Averages cannot tell you anything about the health and well-being of your child.

If you built castles in the air, your work need not be lost; that is where they should be. Now put foundations under them.

HENRY DAVID THOREAU

POINTS TO REMEMBER

■ As a parent, everything that you do will be a model for your child.

■ Being attentive and affectionate with your child will not "spoil" her.

■ You prepare your children for adulthood by teaching them to be resilient and self-confident.

■ The timing of when your child reaches specific milestones says nothing about her potential, overall health and well-being or likelihood of later success.

■ Knowing the facts will help you make an informed decision, one that is right for you.

■ Mothers and fathers can both bond with their child, as well as support and nurture one another.

■ No one can stay in control of their emotions all the time.

■ Every child is unique.

summing up

NOTES

Parenting is hard work. In fact, it is likely the most challenging job you'll ever face. Fortunately, the benefits outweigh the workload. It is unlikely that you will ever reap the rewards and satisfaction from any other undertaking that will compare with those you will derive from being a parent.

It is important for you, on your parenting journey, to reflect often on what you are doing and why. By understanding why you react as you do to specific situations, you can handle them the way that is best for your child. By knowing what is in your parenting tool kit – and having discarded those tools you feel are inappropriate – you can be the parent you want to be. Remember, parenting is an evolutionary process, one that requires you to pick up new skills and insights along the way and use them to your advantage.

Equipped with a sense of humor and faith in your instincts and goals, you can do a good job of parenting. You can work to stay "on your child's side" when addressing behavior issues and can then allow her to become herself. You can nurture your child's uniqueness, intelligence and creativity and allow them to blossom within a relationship of trust, love and respect. And how will you know that you have? By seeing your child grow more aware and more secure in her world. Years from now, when your baby is grown and heading out into the world to make her own way, she will be confident, responsible and well-rounded. The greatest reward will be in the realization that you are continually enjoying the fruits of a strong and positive parent-child relationship.

Working Paper

my goals for parenting

Now that you have completed this book, try to write down some immediate (in the next six months), short term (in the next year) and long term (in the next few years) parenting goals. Discuss these goals with your parenting partner.

Immediate: _____

_____

_____

_____

_____

Short term: _____

_____

_____

_____

_____

_____

Long term: _____

_____

_____

_____

_____

recommended reading

- *Your Baby and Child: From Birth to Age Five,* New Version, by Penelope Leach, New York: Alfred A. Knopf, 1998.

- *Children First: What our society must do - and is not doing – for our children today,* by Penelope Leach, New York: Alfred A. Knopf, 1994.

- *Growing Together: A Parent's Guide to Baby's First Year,* by Dr. William Sears, Franklin, Illinois: La Leche League International, 1998.

- *The Baby Book: Everything You Need to Know about Your Baby – From Birth to Age Two,* by Dr. William Sears and Martha Sears, R.N., New York: Little Brown and Company, 1993.

accreditation

Joyful and Confident Parenting is based on the works of Dr. Penelope Leach and Dr. William Sears.
These works include:

- *Your Baby and Child: From Birth to Age Five*, New Version, by Penelope Leach, New York: Alfred A. Knopf, 1998.

- *Children First: What our society must do - and is not doing – for our children today*, by Penelope Leach, New York: Alfred A. Knopf, 1994.

- *Growing Together: A Parent's Guide to Baby's First Year*, by Dr. William Sears, Franklin, Illinois: La Leche League International, 1998.

- *Becoming a Father: How to Nurture and Enjoy Your Family*, by Dr. William Sears, Franklin, Illinois, Le Leche League, 1998.

- *The Baby Book: Everything You Need to Know about Your Baby – From Birth to Age Two*, by Dr. William Sears and Martha Sears, R.N., New York: Little Brown and Company, 1993.

Editors: Dali Castro and Carol Lawlor

Designers: The Adlib Group and Beth Gorbet

resources for your child's safety

In Canada:
Infant and Toddler Safety Association (ITSA), 385 Fairway
Road South, Suite 4A - 230, Kitchener, Ontario N2C 2N9
(519) 570-0181

In the USA:
Consumer Product Safety Commission (CPSC),
Washington, DC, 20207
(301) 504-0580

The Injury Prevention Program (TIPP) provides
information on accident-proofing your child's
environment. *The Family Guide to Car Seats* lists all
approved car seats. For information on this and other
parenting publications, send a self-addressed stamped
envelope to The American Academy of Pediatrics,
Department C, P.O. 927, Elk Grove Village, Illinois
60009-0927

Resources for Parenting Information:
In Canada:
Canadian Institute of Child Health
384 Bank Street, Suite 300, Ottawa, Ontario K2P 1Y4
(613) 230-8838

In the USA:
I am Your Child Campaign
For further information on parenting resources in your
state, call (888) 447-3400

Look for these ParentSmart Books
at leading bookstores and other retail outlets

Positive Discipline

Some of the most challenging situations for parents and their child involve dealing with discipline issues. Starting with the basic premise that discipline starts with love, this book looks at changing discipline needs, as children go through early stages of development.

Topics covered in *Positive Discipline* include:

- how discipline techniques can affect a child's self-esteem
- the characteristics of positive discipline
- handling your own emotions and anger
- the trouble with spanking
- discipline versus punishment
- avoiding tantrums
- why you can't spoil with love
- setting appropriate limits

This book provides parents with eight practical strategies they can use to encourage cooperation from their children, and sets out easy-to-follow techniques for handling various discipline issues, including tantrums, defiance and anger. There are sections that provide guidance on dealing with discipline problems when a child is living part-time with separated or divorced parents, and on how parents can better manage their own anger, to the benefit of their children and parenting partners.

Your Baby and Child's
Growth and Development

From the moment of conception, a child's rate of growth and development is determined by a complex combination of genetic and environmental factors. This book helps parents to fully understand the factors affecting their baby's growth and development.

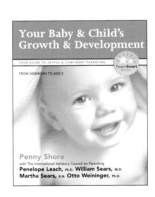

The book is organized into separate sections, each dealing with a particular phase of development, including the first six months and up to preschool. Each section looks at the factors of most concern during the particular period, including weight gain, changes in nutritional requirements, sleep patterns, increased mobility, speech and language development.

Growth and Development provides invaluable guidelines to help parents manage their baby's environment during these first vitally important years.

Topics covered in *Growth and Development* include:

- when to start baby on solid foods
- changing sleep patterns
- physical activities and feelings
- your child in play groups
- what to anticipate at each growth stage
- weight gain
- body awareness
- toddler's self-esteem
- fun and fitness

This book provides parents with an easy-to-follow guide to their baby and child's growth and development.

How Your Baby & Child Learns

Most parents want their child to have a love of learning and to do well in school. Recent research now confirms that there is much that parents can do to provide the care and stimulation which enhances learning in the first few years. *How Your Baby & Child Learns* contains information on numerous subjects, including creating a positive learning environment, a baby's early brain development and dealing with children who have special needs.

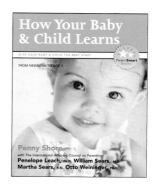

This book explores the stages of a baby's intellectual development. It provides information, as well as tips and techniques, on how parents can stimulate their child's interest in reading and how learning music also enhances mathematical abilities.

Topics covered in *How Your Baby & Child Learns* include:

- how the brain is hard-wired
- learning social responsibility
- numbers and quantitative thinking
- learning through friends
- talking to your baby
- stimulating a healthy curiosity
- talking and listening
- learning through play
- learning by pretending
- toddlers and television
- reading to your child
- music and learning

This book gives parents the information they need to enhance their child's learning opportunities.

Your Baby and Child's
Emotional and Social Development

New research gives us a better understanding of how babies develop emotionally and socially. This book will give parents new insights into these important developmental processes and things they can do to enhance the long term well-being and feelings of security in their child.

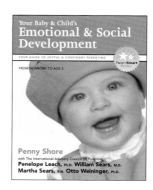

Topics covered in *Emotional and Social Development* include:
- ten strategies for your child's healthy emotional development
- baby's feelings
- what it means when babies cry
- the importance of a baby's gaze
- the child-friendly environment
- the five senses
- toddler socializing
- the parent partnership
- enriching the bond

Readers will learn the timing of emotional development, from the child's initial bonding with the parents, to relating to others outside of the immediate family.

This book is must reading for every parent who is concerned with the emotional and social well-being of their child.

Medical Emergencies & Childhood Illnesses

This book should have a place of importance in every home with small children. No matter how carefully children are supervised, medical emergencies can happen. And when they do happen, this guide provides easy-to-follow procedures.

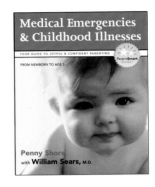

Everything the caregiver needs to know is set out clearly, with instructions on the appropriate course of action. There are three sections in this book: Medical Emergencies, Childhood Illnesses and Your Child's Personal Health Journal. The section on Medical Emergencies covers all of the common situations, including:

- broken or fractured bones
- head and nose injuries
- breathing difficulties
- emergency medical kit
- strains and sprains
- convulsions and seizures
- sunburn
- bites and stings
- choking
- poisoning
- burns
- bleeding
- eye injuries
- shock

A separate section on Childhood Illnesses provides caregivers with an easy-to-understand directory. It includes the symptoms to look for, the action to be taken by the caregiver, as well as an alert on special things to watch for in each particular situation.

The Personal Journal section will provide for an important record of a child's inoculations, illnesses and hospitalizations. It can be used when visiting the family doctor or when traveling.

With children, one thing is certain — illnesses and injuries are inevitable. Having this book conveniently accessible will ensure that information is always available when it is needed.

The International Advisory Council on Parenting

Penny Shore

Created the *ParentSmart Books* and is President of The Parent Kit Corporation. She was Vice President, Product Development for Hume Publishing, and a management consultant with degrees in psychology and gerontology. An expert on the development of home study programs on a variety of topics, Ms. Shore is a parenting educator and an advocate for effective parenting.

Penelope Leach, Ph.D.

Was educated at Cambridge University, London School of Economics and University of London, where she received her Ph.D. in psychology. She is a renowned author of many books, including **Your Baby and Child** and **Your Growing Child**, fellow of the British Psychological Society, past President of the Child Development Society and acknowledged international expert on the effects of parents' different child-rearing styles on children.

William Sears, M.D.

Regarded as one of North America's leading pediatricians, is a medical and parenting consultant to several magazines and organizations, and a frequent guest on television shows. Dr. Sears received his pediatric training at Harvard Medical School's Children's Hospital and Toronto's Hospital for Sick Children. He is the author of many books on parenting, including **The Baby Book** and **The Discipline Book**.

Martha Sears, R.N.

Is a registered pediatric nurse and co-author, with her husband, William Sears, of many books on parenting, including **Parenting the Fussy Baby and the High-Need Child.** In addition to being a regular contributor to several national magazines for parents, she has appeared on more than a hundred television shows and is a popular speaker at parents' organizations across North America.

Otto Weininger, Ph.D.

Served for 15 years as chairman of the Early Childhood Program at the University of Toronto, where he received his Ph.D. in psychology. He is the author of several books including **Time In** and former editor of *The International Journal of Early Childhood Education*. He is a host and frequent guest on radio and television programs around the world, sharing his expertise on children's education, play, learning and relationships.

YOUR PARENTING JOURNAL

Date   **Comments**

YOUR PARENTING JOURNAL

Date   **Comments**

YOUR PARENTING JOURNAL

Date   **Comments**

YOUR PARENTING JOURNAL

Date

Comments

YOUR PARENTING JOURNAL

Date   **Comments**

YOUR PARENTING JOURNAL

Date   **Comments**

index